Forgive us...
as we forgive...

A reflective and practical guide
to putting forgiveness into practice

Pam Pointer

kevin
mayhew

First published in 2003 by

KEVIN MAYHEW LTD
Buxhall, Stowmarket, Suffolk, IP14 3BW
E-mail: info@kevinmayhewltd.com

KINGSGATE PUBLISHING INC
1000 Pannell Street, Suite G, Columbia, MO 65201
E-mail: sales@kingsgatepublishing.com

9 8 7 6 5 4 3 2 1 0

ISBN 184417 145 0
Catalogue No 1500636

Cover design by Angela Selfe
Edited by Graham Harris
Typesetting by Louise Selfe
Printed in Great Britain

Contents

For Jane

Acknowledgements

I'd like to thank:

Roger Pearce for his Bible teaching and permission to use an extract from one of his sermons on page 58.

Jonathan Aitken for his encouragement and letting me quote him on page 39.

Canon David Slater for wise advice based on long experience in Christian ministry and pastoral care.

Thanks are also due to many other friends who, often unknowingly, have got me thinking, questioning and studying and have thus helped frame this book. My family, as ever, have been a collective tower of strength, giving me the occasional kick to keep me going, along with hugs and words of affirmation.

Preface

'I can't call myself a Christian because I can't forgive,' said a friend. Little did my chum realise how those words kept pounding my brain in an unrelenting challenge. I decided to write a little leaflet in response – an attempt to answer some serious questions covering a range of situations involving forgiveness.

These ranged from matters affecting individuals' lives directly at an intimate level, to the broader picture concerning world events affecting us all. At the personal level this meant family tragedy, relationships that had turned sour, and discord among families, friends and colleagues. Globally, events such as 11 September 2001, the overthrow of Saddam Hussein's regime in Iraq and the conflict between Israel and the Palestinians were in my mind.

I soon discovered that forgiveness couldn't adequately be dealt with in a leaflet. I didn't have to look far, however, in my search for some answers, though they sometimes made for uncomfortable reading and honest heart-searching. The Bible has much to say on the subject, not least in The Lord's Prayer and its tricky phrase: 'Forgive us . . . as we forgive . . .'

In the Bible we find problems highlighted, advice, commands and practical help given, but first and foremost, the astonishing and potentially life-changing news that each of us is so loved by God that he wants us to have a relationship with him.

And that's where forgiveness makes its entrance . . .

This book:
- examines the phrase *forgive us . . . as we forgive . . .* in its biblical context and applies it in the twenty-first century;
- draws on biblical teaching on forgiveness using biblical texts;
- heightens awareness of the need for, and availability of, forgiveness.

It may be used for individual study or for a weekly group study over a term. Each chapter consists of:
- an introduction;
- points to ponder;
- Bible reading with comments and questions;
- thought for the day;
- a Bible verse to memorise;
- a prayer.

God's desire is for each of us to lead full lives in a restored relationship with him. I hope that as you read *his* book, the Bible, in conjunction with this book you will come to know him in a fresh and life-changing way and, as a result, will be able to share the resulting joy, peace, grace and forgiveness with others. Join me in this adventure of discovery.

About the author

Pam Pointer's writing includes 'And Finally' for the Diocese of Salisbury's newspaper, *The Sarum Link,* and 'Churches In Focus' for *The Salisbury Journal.* She is a contributor to an international Bible devotional guide, broadcaster of 'Morning Thoughts' for BBC Radio Wiltshire and has written Bible notes for Scripture Union.

Pam's interests include photography, country walking, gardening and collecting weird and wonderful pieces of wood and stone. She is an avid radio listener, watches black and white movies, follows all ball sports except football, and couldn't live without music. She is married to Mike and they have three adult daughters.

Chapter 1

Introduction

Radical relevance

The Lord's Prayer, instigated by Jesus Christ for his disciples, is radical, controversial and as relevant in the twenty-first century as a pattern for prayer as when it was first uttered on a hillside in first-century Palestine.

I gabbled it in rote fashion in school assemblies; few of us understood or appreciated its meaning – it was never explained. Over many centuries it has been chanted or recited in churches; it is used on great national occasions and at christenings, weddings and funerals. Familiarity has sometimes dulled its impact. The Lord's Prayer is worthy of re-examination! If used and applied it could revolutionise not only our prayer life but the living out of that life on planet earth in the twenty-first century.

Stumbling block?

The purpose of this book is to examine one key phrase from the Lord's Prayer, one which proves a stumbling block or an embarrassment for many of us.

'I couldn't call myself a Christian,' a friend told me, 'because I can't forgive.'

'Forgive us our sins, as we forgive those who sin against us.' We might manage to trot out the first four words with confidence, even eagerness, but the next bit reduces our voice box to an inaudible series of reluctant grunts . . . 'Forgive others . . .' an impossibility, a joke, or a challenge?

How to pray

Jesus had been out on the hillside talking to and teaching great crowds of people, pointing them to practical ways of living peacefully with each other. Now he turns to the practicalities of prayer. The people to whom he was speaking were used to praying – they'd been brought up on the Hebrew scriptures where communication with God through prayer was common practice. But he was taking them a leap further.

'When you pray,' Jesus began. Not 'if' you pray, but 'when'. Do you pray? Maybe in a crisis or when someone's ill, maybe never. To whom do you pray, if and when you do? Some vague force for good, the creator of the universe? Jesus himself prayed and encouraged others to do so. So, 'When you pray,' he said, 'say, *Our Father.*' Here was God's Son giving his followers – ordinary mortals – the right to call God, 'Father' – a relational, personal position; moreover, they could call God, '*Our* Father'. What an extraordinary privilege! Jesus was telling people that God wants there to be communication between himself and human beings and that it can take place in the close bond of a personal relationship.

Points to ponder

- When did you first hear the Lord's Prayer? What was your reaction?
- Imagine you were there when Jesus delivered The Sermon on the Mount. What drew you to hear the itinerant preacher – curiosity, physical or emotional need, a spiritual void?
- You have heard about true happiness *(Matthew 5:1-12)*, how to be salt and light *(Matthew 5:13-16)*, teaching about the Law *(Matthew 5:17-20)*, teaching about anger *(Matthew 5:21-26)*, teaching about adultery *(Matthew 5:27-30)*, teaching about divorce *(Matthew 5:31-32)*, teaching about vows *(Matthew 5:33-37)*, teaching about revenge *(Matthew 5:38-42)*, love for enemies *(Matthew 5:43-48)*, and teaching about charity *(Matthew 6:1-4)*. Phew! What a lot to take in. Do you now breathe a sigh of relief? Jesus now gives a practical pattern on how to pray. After all that teaching, you realise how much you need to pray!

Bible reading: Matthew 6:5-13

- When do you pray? In verse 5a Jesus assumes that we do!
- Where do you pray? With reference to verses 5b-6 how might we be hypocritical when we pray? What practical measures can we

take to avoid hypocrisy in prayer? What does the need to be seen suggest about a person's attitude? Why do you choose a particular place for prayer? How does that place affect your attitude, concentration and the content of your prayers?

- What is your preferred posture – standing, sitting, kneeling, arms raised, hands together, hands open? What is helpful to you about your chosen posture? What might be helpful about the suggestion in verse 6?

- What do you say? Are you a chatterbox *(verse 7)* – the sort of person who wants to hide the phone bill when it comes, or a person of few words? Do you share your thoughts or keep them to yourself? Sometimes one of my children would ask me: 'What shall I say?' if they had to go and see a teacher or make a tricky phone call. Think about what you say to your partner, to a child, to a colleague, to a friend. Would you talk in a similar or different way to God?

- So what do we say? The Lord's Prayer tells us! But if you want to develop your relationship with God through prayer you might like to consider using this acronym; **ACTS: Adoration** – if God is worth speaking to, tell him so! **Confession** – tell him about your mistakes, deliberate wrongdoing, unwitting wrongs. **Thanksgiving** – thank him for sunshine, plant and animal life, food, the intricacies of the human form, the birth of a baby. How sad if, at such an awesome time as the birth of a baby, you have no 'higher' being to thank. **Supplication** – a posh word for 'please'. Don't be afraid to ask God – for advice, for needs; share your desires, your dreams and hopes. Remember, he wants to hear us!

If God knows what you need why pray at all? Verse 8 tells us that prayer is part of our relationship with God. Communication between loved ones is vital for a healthy relationship! The supposedly strong, silent type often finds it difficult to communicate in words his deepest feelings; conversely the verbose person can fail to listen because he's too busy talking. How might such attitudes affect us when we pray?

Thought for the day

Praying is a good way of keeping in touch with God. Like the telephone, access is easy and on the other end there is an unseen, listening ear.

Memorise

Turn to the Lord and pray to him, now that he is near. Let the wicked leave their way of life and change their way of thinking. Let them turn to the Lord our God; he is merciful and quick to forgive. *Isaiah 55:6-7*

Prayer

Thank you, God,
    that you listen and understand me.
Thank you for Jesus,
    who taught us how to pray and for the Spirit who prompts us.
Help us to make time for you,
    to learn and live for you and,
    in this tricky matter of forgiveness,
    to be willing to discover what you have to say on the subject,
    and then put it into practice.

Amen.

Chapter 2

Forgive us

Why?

Why do we need to ask God to forgive us? When God created human beings it was because he wanted a relationship with human beings – the pinnacle of his creation process.

> God said: 'Let us make man in our image, in our likeness . . .' So God created man in his own image, in the image of God he created him, male and female he created them . . . God blessed them . . .
> *Genesis 1:26-28*

> God saw all that he had made, and it was very good. *Genesis 1:31*

> The Lord God formed the man from the dust of the ground and breathed into his nostrils the breath of life, and the man became a living being. *Genesis 2:7*

People were created in God's own image. God gave each human being a mind to discern and make choices. Otherwise we would have been automatons – robots primed to do certain things at certain times in certain ways. How dull! A creative creator would want more than that! So human beings were commissioned by God to be good stewards of the created world, to take care of it, even to choose names for the birds and beasts. God valued companionship and recognised man's need for interdependence.

God placed the first human beings into the perfection of his creation where they could enjoy their responsibilities and privileges. They were free to work and derive pleasure in the company of God and one another in a magnificent setting. He gave them free will – with one proviso . . . and they blew it! Disobeying the only prohibition made by God, they then tried to lie their way out of the deception.

Ever since, all human beings have fallen prey to the beguiling tactics of God's enemy, the devil. And it is impossible for flawed people to have a relationship with the perfect God. There is a yawning gulf between God and people. The relationship may only be restored if we ask for, and God grants, forgiveness.

Why should we want a restored relationship with God? Because that is God's purpose for people. We, who have been made in his image, can only be fully human when we have a relationship with the God who created us in that image.

How?

How can we mend the relationship? The bad news is that we can't. But God can. However good we may be, however sincere, however loving, however many charities we support . . . our own efforts are not enough because we are still sinners. Jesus, as God's Son, entered the world as a human being. He knew human nature and he knew God's nature because he was fully human (for the 30 or so years of his life as a man) and also fully God. The Bible teaches that Jesus was there from the beginning of the world. It was his desire to show how much God loves people and he wanted to restore that special relationship. Only a perfect being could be good enough to bridge the gap between us and God. Despite being tempted by the devil while on earth, Jesus never did anything wrong. His perfection resulted in an act that cost him his life. By his sacrificial death, he paid the penalty for our sins. It is we who should have been punished, not him!

When a footballer is shown a red card for a serious offence he has to leave the pitch. He is punished for his misdemeanour. Imagine the referee or manager stepping in and saying: 'I will take the punishment instead.' There would be incredulity, shouts of: 'That's not fair,' and uproar from opposition and crowd alike.

Because of his immense love and longing to forgive and restore that special relationship between God and human beings, Jesus was prepared to shoulder the burden of our sins, and open the way for a restored relationship. Fair? Hardly. But that's the measure of God's perfect love, devotion, desire – and justice. God couldn't just overlook sin and say it didn't matter. It had to be dealt with. Moreover, the resurrection, when Jesus Christ came back to life, was an all time victory over sin, the devil and death itself. The gulf was bridged and nothing could stop the passage of human feet running to the feet of the almighty God, who offers a loving, fatherly relationship and invites us to call him 'Dad'. God reaches out to us and draws us to himself.

Jesus told a great story to his friends. A father had two sons, one of whom wanted to live life in the fast lane. He left home to enjoy wine, women and song and squandered the money his father had given him. The young man ended up penniless, hungry and wretched, eventually deciding to go home and beg to be taken back – even as a servant in his father's house. His father had been watching, wondering and waiting – longing for his son to return to him. One day, looking from his window, he spied the ragged rascal returning. Gathering up the skirt of his long robe, the father ran to meet him. Ran! To Jesus' listeners this was outrageous. What self-respecting Jewish patriarch would run! That is the picture that Jesus painted of God's attitude to any one of us who wants to enjoy a mended relationship with him. He runs to greet us, hugs us and welcomes us home to where we belong. No wonder John Newton wrote of 'amazing grace'! Such gracious love can change our lives, our world view and our destiny.

One way

Forgiveness is available for everyone who asks. There has to be an acknowledgement of need, a belief that Jesus Christ is the way by which we may be forgiven, and a desire to live God's way in future, with his help. Jesus never uttered an untruth. So when he said: 'I am the way,' he meant it. Only he was good enough to unlock the gate of heaven and let us in. There are many ways to Jesus, but he is the only way to God.

Points to ponder

Jesus knew what his purpose was and the immense cost. Imagine, if you can, how he felt at different stages. It might be helpful to read the following Bible passages one at a time, then spend a few minutes in silent contemplation of what it meant to Jesus to do this for you.

Bible reading: Matthew 20:17-19

Jesus sets out determinedly to go the city where he will be killed. How aware am I of what it cost Jesus to die for me?

- Jesus knows of the plots to kill him. Jesus said that whoever is not for him is against him – whose side am I on? *Matthew 26:1-5*
- Jesus knows one of his closest friends will betray him. Am I more interested in money and status than in knowing Jesus? *Matthew 26:14-25*
- Jesus knows his friends will abandon him. Am I willing to show my allegiance to Jesus? *Matthew 26:31-35*
- Jesus' prayer agony. Am I asleep, oblivious, indifferent to what Jesus suffered for me? Am I awake and aware of all Jesus did for me? *Matthew 26:36-46*
- Jesus is tortured and killed. He went through all that – for me. *Matthew 26:67; 27:27-31*

Have I ever acknowledged it?

Thought for the day

Only perfect love could shoulder the colossal burden of the sins of the world. God is love – how else would he be willing and able to forgive us?

Further reading: Matthew 26 and 27

Read the whole account of Jesus' trials and death. Look at all the people involved. With whom do you identify?

- The chief priests and elders – secret plans to kill Jesus;
- The woman with the perfume – worshipping Jesus with a practical gesture;
- Judas Iscariot – betrayer;
- Peter – denied he ever knew Jesus;
- Peter, James and John – too sleepy to support Jesus in his need;
- Disciples – running away from Jesus;
- High priest, teachers of the law and the elders – abused Jesus and tortured him;
- Pilate – washed his hands of Jesus;
- Pilate's soldiers – abused, mocked, tortured and crucified Jesus;
- Passers-by – hurled insults at Jesus.

Memorise

- God loved the world so much that he gave his only Son, so that everyone who believes in him may not die but have eternal life. *John 3:16*
- His death was a sacrifice to bring forgiveness. *Isaiah 53:10b*
- My devoted servant, with whom I am pleased, will bear the punishment of many and for his sake I will forgive them. *Isaiah 53:11b*
- He took the place of many sinners and prayed that they might be forgiven. *Isaiah 53:12b*

Prayer

Lord Jesus,
    I'm sickened by what I read;
    how could they have done all that to you,
    the only perfect person who has ever lived?
But you came for the sole purpose of saving us
    from the sin that taints us.
Were it not for your love
    we could never have a relationship with you,
    because we would not experience your forgiveness.
Teach me what it meant to you, the holy one,
    to take away my sin.

Amen.

Chapter 3

An important digression

Before we go on any further, we need to take a closer look at the person whose prayer we are considering. How can we know Jesus is *the* way? Think of three As: Authority, Approval and Authenticity. Jesus spoke with authority. In the Old Testament Moses heard that God's name is *I am*. He was, is and ever will be who he says he is. Jesus picked up on this when he used the phrase of himself.

> I am the bread of life. He who comes to me will never go hungry, and he who believes in me will never be thirsty. *John 6:35*

> I am the living bread that came down from heaven. If anyone eats of this bread, he will live for ever. This bread is my flesh, which I will give for the life of the world. *John 6:51*

> I am the light of the world. Whoever follows me will never walk in darkness, but will have the light of life. *John 8:12*

> I am the gate for the sheep . . . whoever enters through me will be saved. He will come in and go out, and find pasture . . . I have come that they may have life, and have it to the full. *John 10:9-10*

> I am the good shepherd. The good shepherd lays down his life for the sheep . . . I know my sheep and my sheep know me . . . and I lay down my life for the sheep. *John 10:11, 14-15*

> I am the resurrection and the life. He who believes in me will live, even though he dies, and whoever lives and believes in me will never die. *John 11:25-26*

> I am the way, the truth and the life. No one comes to the Father except through me. *John 14:6*

Such authority is underlined in the opening of John's Gospel, where Jesus is described as 'the Word':

> In the beginning was the Word, and the Word was with God, and the Word was God. He was with God in the beginning. Through him all things were made; without him nothing was made that has been made. In him was life . . . The Word became flesh and made his

dwelling among us. We have seen his glory, the glory of the one and only, who came from the Father, full of grace and truth. *John 1:1-3, 14*

As well as authority, the New Testament abounds in God's approval and affirmation of Jesus as *the* way. On at least two occasions, God's voice was heard by Jesus' followers affirming Jesus as: 'My beloved Son'. And God urged the people to: 'Listen to him'!

Is Jesus authentic? Look at the evidence, listen to the witnesses – at the time and through 2000 years. People of all ages, across every continent, will testify to his validity. Jesus is an unlikely, even absurd candidate to be the Saviour of the world:

> Here is a man who was born in an obscure village, the child of a peasant woman. He worked in a carpenter's shop until he was thirty, and then for three years he was an itinerant preacher. He had no credentials but himself. While still a young man, the tide of popular opinion turned against him. His friends – the 12 men who had learned so much from him, and had promised him their enduring loyalty – ran away, and left him. He went through a mockery of a trial; he was nailed upon a cross between two thieves; when he was dead, he was taken down and laid in a borrowed grave through the pity of a friend.
>
> Yet I am well within the mark when I say that all the armies that ever marched, and all the parliaments that ever sat, and all the kings that ever reigned, put together, have not affected the life of man upon this earth as has this one solitary life. *Anonymous*

There are many ways to Jesus. The Gospels give plenty of examples: the man with a view – from up a tree, the one who came secretly at night, partygoers and party poopers, women of the street via public humiliation. Some met him at weddings, others at funerals, some were desperate, lonely, tired, and life was getting them down; others were living it up. Some came with doubts, others were impulsive, tactile sorts – couldn't wait to touch him, while others hung back. What they had in common was curiosity and need. What is life for? Why am I on this planet? Who is this person whose love is such that he is prepared to die so that I can live? And who claims he can forgive sins?

In order to understand Jesus' prayer let's be open to investigating his life and death. Read one of the Gospel accounts and think of three Cs:

- Consider his Claims;
- Check his Credentials;
- and above all, Contemplate the Cross – the centre of the Christian faith, through which forgiveness and restoration become possible.

The way is open for forgiveness

The Cross on which Christ died spans the gulf between human beings and God. It is not a pretty piece of gold jewellery worn round the neck as a kind of good luck charm. It was a rough piece of wood on which criminals died an agonising, horrific death by slow torture. For Jesus Christ it was much more than physical agony. The open way came at an immense price. It is because Jesus died to pay the penalty for the sins of the whole world that the cross has become the symbol of Christianity. It is a symbol of God's love. The only way for a restored relationship with God was for sin to be dealt with, and God himself, in the form of his sinless son, became that Way. What extraordinary lengths God was prepared to go to in order to rescue us. Such love. And totally undeserved.

So, because of Christ's sacrificial death on the Cross, the way is open for the restored relationship between us and God. God, in his goodness, has taken the initiative. It is his gift to us. We either accept it gratefully, or reject it. There is nothing you or I can do to earn the forgiveness of our sins. Striving to be 'good' is no good. The good news is that God has done it for us through Jesus Christ. Are we prepared to admit our sin, believe in Jesus Christ as Saviour and come to him by faith? It means trusting God and being willing to commit our life to him. And that means changes. We can't go on the way we always have. From now on, we are called to live the life of a forgiven, redeemed person, to live in the light of what Jesus Christ has done for us.

> Praise, my soul, the king of heaven,
> To his feet thy tribute bring,
> Ransomed, healed, restored, forgiven,
> Who like me his praise should sing?
>
> *Henry Frances Lyte, 1793-1847 (Curate in Devon from 1823)*

PS

Once I have recognised and accepted God's plan for dealing with my sin and have embarked on a restored relationship with him, I may be tempted to think I've arrived. In one sense I have – I've been acquitted! I've been freed from the *penalty of sin*. But that isn't the whole story. Someone once said of salvation that it was a three-stage scenario. First, we come to God and accept him as Saviour and ask him to forgive us and restore us as a member of his family, secondly we come to God daily as his followers and ask him to forgive us for the human frailty that makes us continue to do wrong – the *persistence of sin*, and thirdly we look forward to the time when we will become completely free from the *presence of sin*, in heaven. A case of, 'I have been saved, I am being saved, I will be saved'.

Imagine a garden, perhaps one of those television make-over jobs where the expert goes in, spends a fortune and changes an unlikely eyesore into a magnificent array of colour, shape and texture. Initiative has been taken by the master gardener whose plan has come to fruition with love and skill. The garden will not, however, continue in its pristine state on its own. Weeds will emerge and pests will creep in and will take a hold, unless maintenance and improvement measures are taken. Advice will need to be taken – which is a flower, which is a weed, will that creature enhance or destroy? Action is required. So it is with the follower of Christ. We can know the joy of having our lives turned around but must exercise continual vigilance to eliminate the persistent habits and characteristics and ways of behaviour that are not conducive to mature growth as Christians. Any frustration we may feel at this stage may be quashed when we remember that our lives are in that middle stage of being saved – the important initial act of forgiveness through repentance and faith has already been achieved by the master gardener!

A clean canvas

A painter friend envies me my word processor where I can alter pieces of writing, but retrieve what has gone before if I need to. When she is working on a canvas, making alterations and improvements, there is no going back. Once she has painted over a piece of canvas, what is underneath can never be retrieved. So it is with God's dealing with our wrongdoings. Once we have asked for forgiveness, in true penitence, he covers over our past and proceeds to enhance and improve the present.

> I will forgive their wickedness and will remember their sins no more. *Hebrews 8:12*

> Repent, then, and turn to God, so that your sins may be wiped out. *Acts 3:19*

Points to ponder

Many people heard Jesus' words and saw his actions of teaching, preaching and healing. They witnessed his compassion and tenderness, thoughtfulness and love. But they also heard challenging words that they didn't like. His presence provoked different responses. What is your reaction to Jesus?

Bible reading: Luke 4:14-30

- Where did Jesus get his effective power from? *(verses 1, 14 , 18)*
- Look at the reactions of the people:
  News spread about him, he taught and everyone praised him. *(verses 14-15)*
  All eyes were on him, he had people's rapt attention. *(verse 20)*
  All spoke well of him. Imagine the whisperings as he sat down from reading the scroll, but verse 22 tells us that all were amazed at his gracious words. Can this really be the lad who helped his dad with the carpentry, they wondered? *(verse 22)*
- And then, as Jesus challenged them, a sudden change of heart – from praise to protest!
  All the people were furious. *(verse 28)*
  They got up, drove him out of the town and tried to throw him off the cliff. *(verse 29)*
- Read Luke 5:17-26. Here's a hilarious scenario. The bigwigs are gathered to listen to Jesus, cheek by jowl with the common herd who've crammed into the house, not wanting to miss the opportunity of seeing and hearing the travelling teacher.
  Imagine the toffs feeling slightly uncomfortable, squashed, having their feet trodden on, elbows digging into them. People have come a long way for this encounter and they're going to squeeze in if they possibly can.
  What's brought so many? What would compel you to walk miles to see and hear Jesus? Think of the friends of the sick man. What prompted them? Had they already experienced Jesus' love, power and forgiveness, that they wanted to risk aching shoulders, cut hands, the possibility of being had for criminal damage . . . in order to take their friend to Jesus?
  Consider their determination, perseverance, enterprise and faith

at the different stages of the story. Observe the reactions of the people involved. Note Jesus' source of power. What did Jesus do for the sick man? What was his response?

Further reading: Acts 3:1-11,16

- In both cases we read that people went home amazed. Does Jesus amaze you?
- Read again Luke 5:26. 'What marvellous things we have seen today!' is preceded by the people praising God. Do we praise God for who he is, what he has done, what he still does today? Does what we read about make any lasting difference to us? Or do we just say: 'Beautiful singing in church, wonderful preaching, awesome stained glass,' and go home and switch on the telly, have lunch – and carry on, largely unaffected. Jesus came to change lives and make lasting changes.

Thought for the day

You can't compartmentalise Jesus and just take the cosy part that suits you. The follower of Christ receives his love, accepts his challenges, and lives his way.

Memorise

Salvation is to be found through him alone; in all the world there is no one else whom God has given who can save us. *Acts 4:12*

Prayer

Lord Jesus Christ,
   your claims are awesome, your credentials impeccable.
Help me to understand your purpose in coming to our world.
You identified with us but without ever doing wrong.
As the perfect Son of God you have the authority to forgive sins.
May I learn to put my trust in you,
   to have confidence in you and to learn how to live my life for you.
                                                                    Amen.

Chapter 4

Forgive *us*

All tarred with the same brush

Why us? Why not just terrorists, murderers, adulterers, fraudsters . . .
those whose crimes are so heinous as to be sub-human? The Bible
tells us that no one is exempt. Everyone needs to receive forgiveness,
however virtuous we may think we are, however trivial our so-called
sins are compared to the notoriety of those whose misdemeanours
make the headlines. Your neighbour may be a delightful elderly lady
who gives you sweets for your children, waters your garden when
you're away and knits blankets for charities, or you may have the
proverbial, 'neighbour from hell', who abuses you verbally if you
ask him to turn down the volume of his music, lets his dog foul your
garden and beats his wife. Pleasant or unpleasant . . . it makes a
difference to us, but is there any difference as far as God is concerned?

> There is no difference, for all have sinned and fall short of the glory
> of God. *Romans 3:23*

The key word there is God. Of course our relationship with our
fellow human beings is important, but where sin is concerned, it is
firstly our relationship with God that is important. Jesus said that
the greatest commandment is to, 'Love the Lord your God with all
your heart, with all your mind, and with all your soul'. I may not be
a murderer or a thief, I may be faithful to my husband, even go to
church occasionally, but I still fall short when it comes to God. We all
do. We were made to be in a good relationship with God.

Have you ever had a dislocated shoulder, knee or ankle? The
joints in our body are designed to fit together and work together.
When they're dislocated, there is pain, discomfort and disability.
Something has to be done to get them together again so that the relationship between the two parts functions properly. Sin dislocates
each of us from God.

Equally important, however, is the fact that each of us is loved.
God's love and interest is in everyone. God has never made any dis-
tinction on grounds of race, colour, age, gender or anything else.

Why should he? He created people; each is unique; he didn't go in for cloning. Each person is special. Everyone is included in his restoration plan.

> God so loved the world that he gave his one and only Son, that whoever believes in him shall not perish but have eternal life. For God did not send his Son into the world to condemn the world, but to save the world through him. *John 3:16-17*

Inclusive love

That God's love is all-inclusive is evident from Jesus' encounters with people. He mixed with rich and poor, prestigious and outcast, religious and irreligious – and he treated each with respect, dignity and love. No one has ever been too bad, sad or glad to be outside God's forgiveness. It is often those who feel themselves to be bad and beyond the pale who feel most their need of God. Those of us who set our own pattern for living and see no need for God may feel no obligation to him or anyone else as we choose to live for ourselves as we please. The Bible is clear. All, by their wrong-doing, contribute to world malaise. There is personal and corporate responsibility involved. Until that is admitted, an individual cannot know forgiveness and the peace of a right relationship with God. Deep within, there will be unrest in the soul, because our humanity is based on being made in God's image; his stamp is on us, whether acknowledged or not.

The first Christians therefore urged people to:

> Repent, then, and turn to God, so that your sins may be wiped out . . . *Acts 3:19*

> Jesus commanded us to preach to the people and to testify that he is the one whom God appointed as judge of the living and the dead . . . everyone who believes in him receives forgiveness of sins through his name. *Acts 10:42-43*

> Jesus is the atoning sacrifice for our sins, and not only for ours but also for the sins of the whole world. *1 John 2:2*

Act now!

'I'll wait till I'm dying, then ask God for forgiveness,' said a woman in her forties. Death bed forgiveness is certainly available for those who turn to God in repentance just before they move into eternity. The thief on the cross next to Jesus Christ recognised Jesus as the Saviour and was assured of a place in heaven. But Jesus came to give us full life now as well as after death. We don't know how many days we will be on this planet, whether we will reach the statutory three score years and ten. Let's enjoy a forgiven – and forgiving – life while we have the opportunity. The fragility of life is all too evident – the sadness of seeing a loved one taken through cancer, a car accident or even an act of terrorism . . . God has made his offer of forgiveness and life; but it is up to us to choose whether or not to accept that gift. And not to put off the decision.

A promise and a task; a warning and a challenge

Those who accept God's rescue plan have already passed from death to life, but that is no excuse for complacency. Each new follower of Jesus is given a task: to spread the good news!

But if we choose to ignore or reject God's offer of a restored relationship with him, we must accept the alternative: judgement and separation from him. The Bible therefore urges:

> Today if you hear his voice, do not harden your hearts . . .
> *Hebrews 3:7*

> In the time of my favour I heard you, and in the day of salvation I helped you. *2 Corinthians 6:2*

Why wait when you could have full life now?

Points to ponder

We tend to be good at passing judgement on others. Think about the people you've rubbed shoulders with today, or this week. Have you silently sized someone up and found something you didn't like? Someone may have knocked your shoulder in an effort to squeeze onto the rush-hour train . . . a housemate left the bathroom in a mess . . . your neighbour spread some gossip about you . . . you were criticised at work in front of a customer . . . Then there are items in the news: that celebrity is having an affair with someone else's husband . . . that politician is blatantly telling lies . . . and so on . . .

Jesus told us to beware of finding specks in other people's eyes when we have planks in our own!

Bible reading: John 4:1-42

This is high drama. Read it aloud and see the drama unfold!

Not only was Jesus speaking to a woman, he, a Jew, was conversing with a hated Samaritan.

She had come to the well in the heat of the day, perhaps because her reputation led her to avoid the more cool but crowded times. Jesus takes the initiative and asks for a drink, sparking off a fascinating dialogue, resulting in not just one, but many changed lives.

• What words would you use to describe how Jesus treated the woman? With a frown of disapproval? Courteously? Harshly? Gently? Find evidence in the verses.

• Note the progressive reaction of the woman to Jesus and his words from their first meeting to the end of the episode. What were the results of this encounter?

For the woman – in verse 15 she shows a desire to receive from Jesus and in verse 17 an honest admission of her lifestyle. In verse 25 there's a growing thrill that she has discovered the Messiah, and in verse 29 she shows a desire to share the news of Jesus' complete knowledge of the individual.

For the disciples – their reaction was surprise but a lack of curiosity (*verse 27*). In verse 31 there is concern for the physical rather than the spiritual and in verse 33 their thoughts were on the stomach rather than the heart. The fact that John has included the encounter in such detail, however, is an indication that they did recognise that something very special had occurred; perhaps John interviewed the woman who, no doubt, was delighted to tell of her meeting with the Saviour of the world.

For the townspeople – verse 39 shows that there is belief in the Messiah because of one woman's testimony! Perhaps they'd talked with his disciples in town. In verse 40 they show a desire for Jesus to stay with them, even though they knew he would be able to unveil their lifestyles as he had done with the woman. His presence, power and above all his offer of life were irresistible (*verse 41*). Because of his words many more became believers.

For Jesus – verses 8 and 40 show that he took every opportunity to meet people and share the good news of salvation, and verses 39-42 report that lives were transformed and his kingdom extended.

Thought for the day

Jesus knows me through and through, my habits, my relationships, my weaknesses. He still wants to sit down, be with me, have a conversation and see my life changed as I recognise him for who he is.

Memorise

- Jesus said, I have come in order that you might have life, life in all its fullness. *John 10:10b*
- Lord, you have examined me and you know me. You know everything I do; from far away you understand all my thoughts. You see me, whether I am working or resting; you know all my actions. Examine me, O God, and know my mind; test me, and discover my thoughts. Find out if there is any evil in me and guide me in the everlasting way. *Psalm 139:1-3, 23-24*

Prayer

Lord Jesus Christ,
    I realise that, whatever I am like, you are interested in me.
Thank you that you love me despite my failings.
Thank you that you came to rescue me from those failings.
My life is as much in need of transforming as the woman's in the story.
May I be as willing as she was to listen to you,
    to recognise you as my Saviour,
    to turn from my sins,
    know your forgiveness
    and allow you to make the necessary changes in my attitudes,
    my behaviour and my lifestyle,
    so that I can walk in your ways with joy and peace.

                                                                Amen.

Chapter 5

Forgive us *our sins*

The S word

Sin is an offensive and unfashionable word. The dictionary defines it as: 'A transgression of God's known will or principle or law,' and: 'The estrangement from God arising from such transgression.'

In an older version of the Lord's prayer, the word trespasses is used instead of sin, deriving from a thirteenth-century French word, but it means a sin or offence. Other versions of the Lord's Prayer speak of 'debts', as in something – not necessarily money – being owed and of an obligation to pay.

> If we claim to be without sin, we deceive ourselves and the truth is not in us. If we confess our sins, he is faithful and just and will forgive us our sins and purify us from all unrighteousness. If we claim we have not sinned, we make him out to be a liar and his word has no place in our lives. *1 John 1:8-10*

Red or green channel

When you go through customs do you go through the red or green channel? Do you have anything to declare? As far as God and our sins are concerned, there is no choice. We all have something to declare and should head for the red channel. To opt for green is to dupe ourselves. We can't dupe God.

Security checks at airports are more stringent following 11 September 2001. X-ray machines endeavour to detect weapons hidden in luggage – sometimes unsuccessfully. Drug couriers carry their booty inside their bodies to try and avoid detection.

God knows us inside out. He doesn't need x-rays to know that there is sin within us – however well we may try and hide it.

> The Lord does not look at the things man looks at. Man looks at the outward appearance, but the Lord looks at the heart. *1 Samuel 16:7*

> O Lord, you have searched me and you know me . . . you are familiar with all my ways. *Psalm 139:1, 3*

So what is sin? What is wrong in God's eyes?

Rules for living

Centuries ago, at a time when a whole nation had abandoned him to live as they pleased, God instructed Moses to give the people ten rules for living, four of which were concerned with the relationship between God and people, and six of which dealt with relationships between people. They were called The Ten Commandments.

First, God reminded the people that they only came into existence and were sustained in life because of him and he therefore required them to see him, exclusively, as their God. He prohibited the worship of anything or anyone that might usurp his place as God. He wanted his name, indeed his whole being, to be used with respect. And just as he had made the seventh day of the week a day of rest, he wanted his people to keep the seventh day as special, a day on which they could have a break from work and have time to worship. So much for the first four.

Relating these to the twenty-first century how would we score? A majority of the world's population would not claim to put God first in their lives. A whole host of other idols are worshipped – from media celebrities to footballers, shopping, food, the health, shape and tone of the human body, sex, computers, wealth, etc. God's name is continually abused and misused and we live in a fast, 24-hour, seven days a week whirl of work, pleasure and leisure.

Do we fare any better in our relationships with people? The other six of God's ten commandments deal with human relationships: honour parents, respect the sanctity of life and marriage, don't take what doesn't belong to you, don't malign your neighbour and don't covet possessions or people that don't belong to you. Sounds straightforward?

Jesus said we only have to think wrong thoughts and it's sin. He summarised the ten commandments like this:

> Love the Lord your God with all your heart and with all your soul and with all your strength and with all your mind, and love your neighbour as yourself. *Luke 10:27*

How do I measure up?

Can any of us, in all honesty, say we have always complied with that? It has been said: 'Love God and do as you like.' There is truth in those words if loving God equates to giving him honour in the way we live, pleasing him in our thoughts, words and behaviour and striving to live to his standards. 'Doing what we like' is then an outworking of an inner resolve to trust and obey God. But paying lip service to loving God while continuing on our chosen lines of behaviour cannot ever be construed as loving God. If we are to follow Jesus' command to love God we have to find out what his code of conduct for our lives is – and adhere to it.

God is not a kill-joy. His rules are in our best interests, a highway code for the pilgrim path. If motorists were allowed to pass the driving test without any knowledge of, or adherence to *The Highway Code*, there would be chaos on the roads. Commands would be ignored and there would be no recognition of warning signs. We know what happens when traffic lights are out of action or when red lights are jumped, how cars and people are damaged when drivers don't give way. Supposing that drivers didn't bother about keeping to the correct side of the road. On the whole, rules of the road are respected and obeyed. God wants us to lead fulfilled lives; his code of conduct is to help us achieve that. The pilgrim's road is hazardous. God can help us to avoid the hazards.

In order to live God's way it is necessary to study and apply his conduct for living. We find this in the Bible – instructions for living now and for preparing for eternity. But always there is the choice. It is up to each of us to decide who we will serve – God, other objects of desire or ourselves.

Caught in the act

Jesus was in the temple in Jerusalem with a crowd of people listening to him teach. Heads turned at a sudden commotion on the edge of the crowd as a group of religious and legal leaders pushed a woman forward to take centre stage with Jesus. 'Look at her,' they screamed at him, 'This adulteress. Caught in the very act. You know what this means – she must be stoned to death!'

How would Jesus react? Everyone waited with bated breath. Were they disappointed that he didn't rant and rave at the woman?

Were the VIPs expecting praise for their diligence in bringing her for punishment? Jesus bent over and wrote with his finger in the dust on the ground. They continued to harangue him with questions as he wrote. Calmly, he straightened up. 'If any of you is without sin,' he said, 'let him be the first to throw a stone at her.' And he bent down again to write on the ground. The Bible doesn't tell us what Jesus wrote. How tantalising! Maybe he scrubbed it out with his foot before anyone else could read it.

One by one, the crowd melted away as they heard Jesus' words. When he stood up again, no one was left except the woman. 'Where are they?' he asked her, 'Has no one condemned you?' 'No one,' she replied. 'Neither do I condemn you,' Jesus declared.

The woman knew what it was to have her past wrongdoing forgiven. But there was an important sequel to the encounter. Jesus, as God's Son, forgave the woman and let her go on her way, freed from the penalty of death but freed to live a new life: 'Go now,' he said, 'and leave your life of sin.' Forgiveness from God involves repentance – a turn around, a change of direction for life.

The crowd didn't have a leg to stand on, so legged it. They knew, deep down, that they were as guilty as the woman they had humiliated.

All wrongdoing is sin. *1 John 5:17*

Life-saver for fatal disease

We may think there are degrees of sin, that some are worse than others. That may be so. We like to categorise and prioritise and to make judgements, but personal inclinations and opinions may be a wobbly base. It is not our place to judge others. Sin is sin. God hates sin in any form because he is sinless. Only God is in a position to mend our broken relationship with himself, caused by our sins. In his love, grace and mercy he has chosen to do so. But at a price.

> Christ suffered for you, leaving you an example, that you should follow in his steps. He committed no sin, and no deceit was found in his mouth. When they hurled their insults at him, he did not retaliate; when he suffered, he made no threats. Instead, he entrusted himself to him who judges justly. He himself bore our sins in his body on the tree, so that we might die to sins and live for righteousness; by his wounds you have been healed. *1 Peter 2:21-24*

Why would anyone do that for someone else? Why would the only perfect man who ever lived, give up his own life? Christ's death was more than that of a martyr. We need to return to the motive: God's love, which was so immense that he was prepared to go to the limit in order to rescue us from our sins and separation from himself.

> Christ died for sins once for all, the righteous for the unrighteous, to bring you to God. *1 Peter 3:18*

It was God's purpose to restore the relationship between himself and his beloved human race. So, by entering the world of humanity himself, he not only showed us the way to live, but was the way to life.

> Wilt thou forgive that sin where I begun,
> Which is my sin, though it were done before?
> Wilt thou forgive those sins, through which I run
> And do them still: though still I do deplore?
> When thou hast done, thou hast not done,
> For, I have more.
>
> *John Donne 1572-1631 (English poet)*

Once we have grasped the enormity of sin, and the enormity of God's saving plan of action, and have come to the point of recognising our need for forgiveness, we are in a position of hope for the next section of the phrase: 'Forgive us our sins, as we forgive those who sin against us.'

Points to ponder

'He started it, Miss!' 'She hit me first, Sir!' 'Mummy, he snatched my toy!' 'I didn't do it, honest!' How many times have we heard such words; attempts to wriggle out of wrongdoing, trying to apportion blame elsewhere, not facing up to our own misdeeds. Adults are as susceptible as children to this denial of sin, to the breaking of the God-given rules for living. 'Forgive us our sins,' Jesus told us to pray, not: 'Forgive us if we have sinned.'

Bible reading Luke 18:9-14

This must be one of the scariest stories Jesus told. He knew that some of his listeners thought they were beyond reproach, self-confident in their own goodness and looking with disdain at other people. So Jesus told this short, sharp story.

- Who were the main characters? Verse 10 – a Pharisee was a top-notch religious leader, the equivalent of a leading churchman today. A tax collector had one of the most despised occupations – someone who collaborated with the hated authorities to extract money from local people. Perhaps traffic wardens or rent-collectors would fall into that category. They know they are loathed for the job they do. Incidentally, a recent, albeit unscientific survey in the UK found that doctors, nurses and teachers are seen as the most worthy workers, and bottom in the popularity stakes are members of Parliament and journalists!
- What was the attitude of the Pharisee? *(verses 11 and 12)*
- Why was the Pharisee so confident?
- What had the Pharisee, for all his religious knowledge and experience, failed to recognise? *(see verse 11, and check out Romans 3:10-18, 23)*
- What was the attitude of the tax-collector? *(see verse 13)*
- Why did he stand at a distance? Why did he hang his head? Why did he beat his breast? Why did he plead for mercy?
- Look at Titus 3:3-7. How does my idea of self-righteousness contrast with God's idea of righteousness? How might we be 'foolish, disobedient, deceived and enslaved'? *(verse 3)* In contrast look at Jesus' attributes and actions. *(verses 4-6)* Think of times when you have known God's 'kindness and love' for you. What process is it necessary for us to go through before we can be saved from our sins? *(verse 5)* Have you acknowledged his mercy *(verse 5)*, his generosity *(verse 6)*, his grace *(verse 7)*, and the fact that he died to save you from your sins? *(verse 5)* What are the results of being put right with God by his righteousness, in contrast to our self-righteousness? *(verses 5 and 7)*
- Do I resemble the Pharisee or the tax-collector?

Thought for the day

Our sins are a fact. So is God's solution. I have a choice: self-righteousness or God-righteousness.

Memorise

God puts people right through their faith in Jesus Christ. God does this to all who believe in Christ, because there is no difference at all: everyone has sinned and is far away from God's saving presence. But by the free gift of God's grace all are put right with him through Christ Jesus, who sets them free. *Romans 3:22-24*

Prayer

Jesus, your story hits a raw spot.
How easy it is to pretend, in arrogant self-righteousness,
    that I'm really a pretty good person
    when you make it clear that I'm not.
Help me to realise that I am no better than the next person,
    that we are all guilty of sin,
      but that you have provided an opportunity for us
      to be cleared of that guilt and to be washed clean.
I come to you and ask for mercy
    and thank you that my life can be transformed because of you.
                    Amen.

Chapter 6

Forgive us our sins *as*

Little and good

Someone once said that we can only begin to forgive when we have received and experienced forgiveness from God ourselves. The two phrases, 'Forgive us . . .' 'we forgive . . .' are linked by that little word, 'as'. They work in harmony. It is as we daily recognise with gratitude, amazement and humility, the grace, love, compassion and mercy of God, that we can begin to learn how to move forward in our attitude to others. The second greatest commandment, Jesus said, is: 'Love your neighbour as you love yourself.'

> You ought certainly to forgive them as a Christian, but never to admit them in your sight, or allow their names to be mentioned in your hearing. *Jane Austen 1775-1817, English novelist* (From *Pride and Prejudice*)

With delicious Austen irony, the author of *Pride and Prejudice* hits on the raw spot; we may have very laudable attempts at forgiveness – and then add a 'but'. Are we prepared, as is God, to wipe the slate clean . . .?

As we come to God through Christ there is a sense of awe and of peace and joy.

> Since we have been justified through faith, we have peace with God through our Lord Jesus Christ, through whom we have gained access by faith into this grace in which we now stand. *Romans 5:1-2*

> Just at the right time, when we were still powerless, Christ died for the ungodly. Very rarely will anyone die for a righteous man, though for a good man someone might possibly dare to die. But God demonstrates his own love for us in this: While we were still sinners, Christ died for us. *Romans 5:6-8*

The blood donor

Many years ago when I worked at St Mary's Hospital in London, I passed, every day, words from John's Gospel that were carved in stone beneath the grand staircase in the main building: 'Greater love hath no man than this: that a man lay down his life for his friends.' Jesus Christ spoke those words to his disciples shortly before his crucifixion. Jesus Christ was prepared to die for a friend who would deny his existence, for another who wouldn't believe Jesus' resurrection unless he saw the nail wounds for himself, for someone who would betray him for money, for a couple of firebrand brothers who argued about where they would sit in heaven, for people who spat at him, tortured him, hammered nails through his hands and feet, lashed his back with a whip, taunted him, rammed a thorny crown onto his head, for people who hated him for overturning their traditions and radicalising their religion and elevating the status of women, lepers, tax collectors. Worst of all, in the eyes of the religious leaders of the day, this Jesus claimed to forgive sins. How dare he! Death was too good for him.

Christ's response from the cross was to call out,

> Father, forgive them, for they do not know what they are doing.
> *Luke 23:34*

Greater love hath no man . . .

Mother Teresa said that we cannot forgive unless we know that we need forgiveness, and that forgiveness is the beginning of love. God can't fill what is full. When we are full of sin, we need forgiveness, to be emptied of self and filled – with God, by God.

There has to be a response when we have accepted God's forgiveness. So, we have the little word, 'As'.

> Amazing grace! How sweet the sound
> That saved a wretch like me!
> I once was lost, but now am found,
> Was blind, but now I see.
>
> *John Newton 1725-1807*

Own up or cover up

Accepting God's salvation and forgiveness means a new direction and a changing life. This includes forgiving others as God in Christ has forgiven me. His love for me leads to his love in me. He becomes Lord of my life; his Holy Spirit within me teaches me and prompts me to live as someone who is in relationship with God. As I begin to take on Christ-likeness, albeit slowly and with setbacks en route, one of the things I have to learn is to forgive others, as God forgives me.

There is the important initial forgiveness by God of my sins when I accept his gift of salvation and embark on the pilgrim route, then there is the daily seeking of forgiveness when I tell my heavenly Father of my wrongdoing that day. Keeping short accounts with God will help us to keep short accounts with other people.

When I was a child and did something wrong at home – scribbling on the wall or deliberately flouting a house rule by continuing to hit tennis balls against the back windows, my first instinct on seeing my graffiti or a broken window pane was to try and cover up. It rarely worked. Parents have an uncanny knack of knowing when something is amiss, even if we do try and hide the evidence. Sometimes I felt defiant, sometimes guilty, occasionally remorseful, but always uneasy, wondering whether – or more likely, when – I would be found out. Until I confessed, the relationship with my parents was diminished; there was a barrier between us. Perhaps they could see it in the way I behaved. They might ask: 'What's the matter?' giving me the opportunity to own up. Eventually, if I failed to own up, I would be quizzed, gently, and the truth would ultimately come out, and there would be a sense of . . . relief! It was out in the open. How much more straightforward if I had owned up straightaway. There might have been a reprimand, an order to clean up or make a pocket money contribution towards repairs, and a caution not to do it again, but once I had said sorry – and meant it – all would be forgiven and the strained relationship restored. Through it all, my parents continued to love me – there was never any question about that, but the relationship was always best when there were no barriers between us.

So it is with God. His love knows no bounds but we create a barrier if our daily shortcomings are not confessed. He is able to forgive and to give us confidence and courage to keep going on the learners' route to heaven.

Forgiveness takes place in the context of relationship. The Lord's Prayer, though used by many as a set, national prayer, was given originally to those who were already in a relationship with God, who already knew his forgiveness, as people who had rejected their former life, repented and resolved to live in a new, restored relationship with the God they could now call Father. The more we experience the forgiveness of God in our lives, the more able we should be to practise generous Christ-likeness; this means a new relationship with other people and a noticeable and active willingness to forgive. Forgive us . . . *as* we forgive.

Points to ponder

As – the joining together of two phrases, two ideas, two actions, an on-going, continuous process.

Reciprocate – following an example, emulating admirable qualities, receiving and giving: continuous circle, one being the result of the other; in the same way that . . .

Bible reading: Matthew 14:1-33

What an extraordinary chapter. Here we have three diverse episodes in the life of Jesus and his disciples. In the first section *(verses 1-12)* we read the horrendous account of the death of John the Baptist at the whim of a princess who twists her father round her little finger. He indulges her and orders the beheading of John, whose head is brought on a platter for the ghoulish princess to ogle at.

* How do you think Jesus felt? What did he do? *(verse 13)* What do you imagine he did in that 'solitary place'?

* What was his reaction when he saw the crowds following him? *(verse 14)* What would have been your reaction in Jesus' circumstances at that time of grief?

* After the healing session, Jesus demonstrates his compassion yet again and feeds 5000 people. Contrast Jesus' attitude with that of the disciples. *(verses 15-19)*

* Once the crowd had gone home, what did Jesus do? *(verse 23)* There are many instances in the Gospels that tell us that Jesus prayed. If he needed to pray, how much more should we!

It had been a very long day; the disciples were out on the lake, being buffeted by the wind and waves. Jesus, after his prayer time, came to them, walking on the water.

* What was their immediate reaction? *(verse 26)*

* Examine the different stages of Peter's reaction in verses 28, 29, 30 and 33.

Peter wanted to emulate Jesus. He was an impulsive character, full of bravado at first, but crumbling under pressure, buoyant with faith one moment, sinking with doubt the next.

If this is your experience, take comfort and strength from Jesus – and follow his example! Here is a classic 'as' scenario.

Jesus experienced grief following John the Baptist's death. He gave himself space, sought solace with the only totally trustworthy source – his Father. Strengthened, he demonstrated the love, compassion and provision of his Father. While the disciples panicked about picnics, Jesus put his own needs on the back burner to care for others.

Thought for the day

Jesus invites people to come to him, looking into his face with faith. When we cry out to him, he reaches down with his hand to lift us up. He climbs into the boat on the storm-tossed sea of life and calms things down. And we worship him.

Memorise

- Christ himself suffered for you and left you an example, so that you would follow in his steps. *1 Peter 2:21*

- We who have found safety with him are greatly encouraged to hold firmly to the hope placed before us. We have this hope as an anchor for our lives. It is safe and sure. *Hebrews 6:18b-19a*

Prayer

Lord Jesus,
    when I have that sinking feeling,
    help me to look to you.
Help me to be part of that circle of trust and obedience,
    holding on to you, reaching out to others,
    returning to you for sustenance, comfort and courage,
    then reaching out again, and again.
Lord Jesus,
    I can only do that effectively if you are truly Lord of my life.
Make me willing to submit to you.

Amen.

Chapter 7

As *we forgive*

> If a man will begin with certainties, he shall end in doubts; but if he will be content to begin with doubts, he shall end in certainties.
>
> *Francis Bacon, 1561-1626 (English lawyer, courtier, philosopher and essayist)*

I fell into that trap! I was pretty sure of what it meant to be forgiven by God, so wrote the first part of this little book with confidence. Then I reached the second part . . . and my certainties turned to questioning. Without doubt, the human action required in forgiving is very hard! No wonder Jesus urged us to ask God the Father for help!

Is it possible to have a forgiving nature without knowing God's forgiveness? Yes, in part. Because we are made in the image of God, we are endowed with his attributes but they can only become fully utilised as God works in the lives of those who have turned to him, received his forgiveness and have begun the pilgrim route with him as their Lord and leader. Nevertheless we are all capable of giving and receiving acts of kindness, forgiveness and acceptance because of the God trait in us all. Former MP, Jonathan Aitken, spoke of 'the milk of human kindness amongst the fraternity of the fallen', that he encountered when in prison for perjury.

Effort

However, because of our fallen human nature, it is also evident that there is an urge within us to feel disappointment, hurt, bitterness, anger and resentment and to have an intransigent unforgiving spirit – when it suits us, or when the hurt is so horrendous that we cannot forgive.

We expect so much of each other! How easily we feel let down by a friend or member of the family. A teenager commented ruefully: 'The worst thing is not so much doing something wrong as having your parents say they're disappointed in you, or even knowing their unspoken disappointment.' Do you know the disappointment of having an anniversary overlooked, the hints about booking a holiday ignored or the humiliation of being put down in front of someone else? Disappointments spill into the distress of hurt and resentment and before we know it, are blown into dark layers of rain clouds where once there was just a wisp of white. Have we never disappointed a friend, let down a colleague, spoken harshly to our child, spiked our spouse?

It's curious how, knowing that each of us is imperfect, we nevertheless expect perfection – or as near as can be – from those around us. It's illogical, impossible and imposes unnecessary grief. We need to return again and again to God's attitude towards us – loving acceptance of us as we are. He hates sin but never stops loving the sinner. Why else would he have chosen such a path of reconciliation as he did?

> Dear Lord and Father of mankind,
> Forgive our foolish ways,
> Reclothe us in our rightful mind,
> In purer lives thy service find,
> In deeper reverence, praise.
>
> *John Greenleaf Whittier 1807-1892 (American poet)*

It is only God's Spirit at work in us – if we allow him to – that can transform our attitudes and put his forgiving nature in us. God, through Jesus Christ, the sinless one, forgives those who turn to him. Only God can forgive sins and give us the gift of a new life, but his grace in us can help us to be more forgiving of other people. Are we willing to be patient, tolerant, long-suffering? We're good at seeing fault in others while ignoring our own faults. Jesus spoke about planks and specks of sawdust and warned of hypocrisy. Let's be ready to say we're sorry and ask forgiveness of those whom we have hurt, and be humble enough to take an olive branch when it's held out to us. The Bible doesn't tell us to be peacekeepers. It tells us to be peacemakers. Effort is involved. There has to be a willingness on our part.

Paul wrote to Christians in Rome about his own struggles:

> I do not understand what I do. For what I want to do I do not do, but what I hate I do . . . I know that nothing good lives in me, that is, in my sinful nature. For I have the desire to do what is good, but I cannot carry it out . . . *Romans 7:15-18*

He describes himself as, 'a wretched man'. But, having turned to live for Christ, he reminds his readers that he – and they – have God's Spirit living in them who can transform them to become more like Christ.

> The Spirit helps us in our weakness. *Romans 8:26*

Courtesy

From the time they learned to speak, our children were taught the importance of three words: Please, thank you, and sorry. The idea was that these courtesies would become a lifetime habit – not to be said glibly, but with real meaning. Do we recognise when we have hurt someone – by something we have said or done, or by thoughts that turn into scowls? How prepared are we to say sorry, and mean it? Unless and until there is genuine remorse and a humble spirit within me such that I am prepared to say 'I'm sorry', I'm going to find it hard to be forgiving towards others. Hard hearts, bitter thoughts, twisted and exaggerated feelings of being hard done by will do nothing to aid peacemaking. Intransigence and a desire for revenge start in the mind and can quickly descend to the heart and hands. It is a slippery slope.

When Paul wrote to the Philippian church he challenged them to look to the interests of others and challenged them to have the same attitude that Jesus Christ had:

> Who, being in very nature God . . . made himself nothing, taking the very nature of a servant . . . he humbled himself and became obedient to death – even death on a cross. *Philippians 2:6-8*

Gracious!

Jesus told the story of a man who owed a vast sum of money to a king. He deserved to be punished; the king ordered him, his wife and children to be sold as slaves along with all that they possessed, and in that way for the debt to be met. The man begged for mercy and the king, feeling sorry for him, forgave him and let him go. He was a free man, free from the threat of slavery, free from his debts, free to make a fresh start with his family. But what happened? Even as he was freed, he grabbed another man who owed him a trifling sum, throttled him and had him thrown in jail till he could pay up.

The king heard about it and called in the first man for a severe talking-to. 'I showed you mercy and forgave you for all that you owed me, and what did you do?' The unforgiving man was thrown in jail and the order was given that he should stay there till he'd paid off the enormous debt. Jesus told this story in response to a question from one of his disciples. Peter had asked him: 'How many times must I forgive a brother? Will seven times be enough?' Did Peter's heart sink when Jesus told him: 'No, seventy times seven.'?

> As God's chosen people, holy and dearly loved, clothe yourselves with compassion, kindness, humility, gentleness and patience. Bear with each other and forgive whatever grievances you may have against one another. Forgive as the Lord forgave you. *Colossians 3:12-13*

It's not unreasonable that Christians are meant to forgive one another (hard though it can be) but are we all meant to forgive anyone anything in any circumstances? Perhaps, sometimes, it has to be a case of letting go. Holding on to our grievances simply chews us up inside and achieves nothing. If we are able to let go, say to God: 'Lord, I'm finding forgiveness in this instance a real struggle. Help me to give it to you, to release the baggage on my back that is bowing me down . . .' he will shoulder it for us and we can walk upright and the backache will subside. Let go, and let God . . . peace will follow and one day you'll realise that you have forgiven and even forgotten. A word of warning though! We have a habit of picking up the bag again. Resist!

> A man that studieth revenge keeps his own wounds green.
>
> *Francis Bacon 1561-1626 (English lawyer, courtier, philosopher and essayist)*

A boiling pot

My brother and I used to squabble and then tell tales to Mum. More often than not she would say: 'That's the pot calling the kettle black.' I had little idea what she meant though it usually shut us up! Our pots, pans and kettles were all silvery and shiny, but visiting a country museum years later I saw an old hearth with its huge, blackened kettle and massive, black cooking pot – and understood. Yes, sometimes both parties are in the wrong and there needs to be mutual confession and forgiveness. Are you the first to say sorry, or do you seethe and mutter behind gritted teeth: 'I'm not going to say sorry till he does!'

Sometimes at Christmas I make fudge. Recipe books warn that you need a large pan. Do I heed the warning? I do now. One year I weighed the ingredients, thought it didn't look much and chose a smallish saucepan. All was well to start with. I melted the ingredients over a gentle heat, then turned up the heat. The mixture fizzed round the edges then began to spatter in the middle; before long a rolling boil was sending up thick gloop in furious bubbles. The heat was searing, the splashes scalding until, without warning the whole thing erupted in a final fling of violence, spilling over the edges of the pan and leaving a frightful mess over the cooker, the worktop and the floor.

We mustn't allow resentment to get a hold. What starts as an internal murmuring erupts into a festering monster that quickly gets out of control and does much damage.

Working for peace

We hear stories sometimes of people who have forgiven perpetrators of crime. In Northern Ireland there's a man whose daughter died when a bomb was detonated at an Armistice Day service. He forgave the killers. In the United States another man whose daughter was blown up in the Oklahoma bombing later made contact with the killer and his family in a process of reconciliation and healing.

We long for peace on earth. Let there be peace on earth and let it begin with me, we might pray. Peace on earth can't begin with me, or you, or any other person. It began a long time ago with God. Into a world of turmoil and rejection of him, he sent his Son as the Prince of Peace. Through him and by knowing his presence in our hearts, we can begin to catch a glimpse of what it means to be peacemakers. With his help, and as we experience his forgiveness of us, we can begin to look on others with the peacemaking qualities of Jesus Christ.

In his will is our peace. *Dante Alighieri 1265-1321 (Italian poet)*

In many churches there is a section in the service known as The Peace. The worship leader says: 'The peace of the Lord be with you,' and the people reply: 'And also with you.' And we are invited to, 'share the peace'. Handshakes or pecks on the cheek are exchanged with a mumbling of the phrase: 'The peace of the Lord . . .' There might or might not be eye contact, there might be a longer conversation. Is it a meaningless ritual? If someone said: 'Peas and carrots,' instead, would you be amused, offended, or not even register? Many of the New Testament letters begin with the greeting: 'Grace, mercy and peace be with you.' Do we really wish God's peace on our fellow-worshippers? Have we experienced his peace in a way that overwhelms us so much that we want it to shower down on our companions, too?

Blessed are the peacemakers. *Matthew 5:9*

Points to ponder

There can be no better example to follow than that of Jesus Christ when considering forgiveness. Only he who asked his Father to forgive his murderers could tell us, when we pray, to say: 'Forgive us . . . as we forgive.' But on a practical level how do we deal with forgiving others?

Bible reading: Matthew 12:15-21

Jesus' ministry spanned just three brief years. During that time he met all sorts of people in different circumstances in places as diverse as synagogues, cornfields, beaches and in the streets of villages, towns and the great city of Jerusalem. He was busy preaching and teaching, healing and comforting, preparing himself and his friends for what lay ahead, always focused on the task in hand – his role as Saviour.

* Look at the context of this passage in chapters 10, 11 and 12.

  Jesus had been giving detailed instructions to his disciples before sending them off on a preaching mission of their own. He knew only too well the responses they might get. At the same time John the Baptist was in prison and Jesus took time to reiterate John's message, urging the people to not just hear the message but act on it.

* Read Matthew 11:16-21 and note how perceptive Jesus is; he points out how people looked at John and subsequently at Jesus himself and passed judgement on them both.

* In Matthew 11:20-24 Jesus reproached the towns where his message was ignored – a warning to those of us who hear but ignore the offer of salvation.

- In Matthew 11:25-28 Jesus turns once more to prayer. Did he sometimes despair of people? He was vocal and active in speaking and living out the good news, but time and again it was ignored. At the same time Jesus saw the needs of people: the burdens of anxiety, problems, guilt, fear, tiredness, and he longed to relieve them of them!

- What does his invitation say? Look at Matthew 11:28-30 and think about your response.

    Some time later Jesus is walking in the fields on the Sabbath and infuriates the Pharisees with his seeming blasphemy about David and Moses. Jesus was challenging long-held and often rigid attitudes that had more to do with tradition than true worship. Jesus then went to a synagogue and healed a man – on the Sabbath.

- What did the Pharisees do? See Matthew 12:14. This is the context of the passage we're looking at!

- If you or I had been Jesus how would we have reacted to the rejection, indifference and hatred that we've noted? What did he do? *(Matthew 12:15)* Is there a time when it is better to withdraw from a tense situation rather than be confrontational? We know that Jesus often withdrew from the crowds to go and pray alone. If you and I are to forgive others, it is unlikely we will be able to do so in our own strength.

    On this occasion crowds followed Jesus and he healed them. Notice how he didn't want to draw attention to himself. Today the most effective preachers and healers are more concerned about pointing people to God than being in the limelight themselves.

- Look at the quotation from Isaiah in verses 18-21. These are the words of God the Father spoken through the prophetic message of Isaiah.

- What was Jesus' role? *(verse 18)* Can you think of instances in the Gospels where he became like a servant?

- To whom did Jesus belong? *(verse 18)*

- What did God say of Jesus? Find three affirming phrases in that same verse.

- How was Jesus going to fulfil his role? *(verse 18b)*

- Read verses 19-20 and ask yourself: 'If I follow Jesus' example and forgive others, what will need to characterise my thoughts, words and actions?'

Thought for the day

Jesus taught us to pray, Forgive us . . . as we forgive. His is the supreme example of a gentle, loving and forgiving nature. His actions pointed to God the Father whose love knew no bounds, to the extent of sending his beloved Son to die to take away my sins.

Further reading

Jesus washes his disciples' feet. *John 13:1-17*

Jesus asks God to forgive his murderers. *Luke 23:26-43*

Memorise

Be tolerant with one another and forgive one another whenever any of you has a complaint against someone else. You must forgive one another just as the Lord has forgiven you. *Colossians 3:13*

Prayer

Lord Jesus,
　　it is only when I look in detail at your life and death
　　that I realise the extent to which you love me.
As I come to you for forgiveness,
　　may I be willing to not just accept you as my Saviour
　　but to have you as Lord of my life.
I want to demonstrate, by being forgiving,
　　that I know your forgiveness.
May my joyful thankfulness always point people to you.
Amen.

Chapter 8

Those who sin against us

Global ghastliness

Since 11 September 2001 there has been a heightened sense of the world as a small place where actions in one place have repercussions for people everywhere. War in Iraq, acts of terrorism elsewhere and continuing conflict in many parts of the world underline such awareness. Modern media coverage brings vivid images into our living rooms. Do they make us think more seriously about life and death, our fragility, mortality and the uncertainty of life? What is our response to the perpetrators of violent acts? Are we shaken out of our comfortable armchairs and languid stupor by what we see? We may have a kind of spiritual yawn, even acknowledge that these acts may be a wake-up call to mend our ways. But despite being able to see and hear more of global happenings than ever before, we soon sink back into our chairs.

There is no lasting cessation of feelings of suspicion, words of hatred and acts of violence. Israel and the Palestinians, Northern Ireland, Indonesia, Zimbabwe . . . and, closer to home, fisticuffs at football matches. In each scenario the individuals affected have to confront the subject of forgiveness for 'those who sin against us'. We long for peace but strife continues. It is not possible for fallen humans to pick themselves up by their shoe laces and overcome sin. It will rise and rise again.

Do we pray for the perpetrators of terrorist attacks? Why pray for evil people? They don't deserve our prayers! But the Bible tells us to pray for those who persecute us. By remembering that none of us is exempt from deserving punishment for our sins but also remembering that, by God's grace, his salvation is open to all, it is right to pray in that way. God loves every human being and longs to have a right relationship with every terrorist who has ever stalked the earth . . .

> We all stumble in many ways. If anyone is never at fault in what he says, he is a perfect man, able to keep his whole body in check. *James 3:2*

47

Nearest and dearest?

Who hurts you most? Sometimes it is the person closest to us – our best friend, partner, child, parent.

Shirley had kept some half-dozen letters she had received from her father over a period of many years. He had left home when she was eight years old. He had served in France during World War I, returned to his family in England and struggled through the slump of the 1920s. Shirley didn't know the reasons for his departure – her older sister said there had been arguments, but wouldn't elaborate. Contact between father and daughters, at first spasmodic and never face to face, dwindled to nothing until, on her twenty-first birthday Shirley received a remorseful letter from her father who assured her of his continuing love.

Some years later Shirley married and her husband encouraged Shirley to keep the tenuous contact with her father alive. The two men never met, but a bridge had been built and gradually the hurts became less painful – Shirley's for the father who had left her and who she never really knew, the father's for his abandonment of his family and the pain of not seeing his children grow up. The family had all been affected by the breakdown in relationship. Shirley's mother struggled as a single mother, the older sister had to be the breadwinner, and Shirley was left with a load of unasked questions, to many of which she never discovered an answer.

The last letter from father to daughter was one of hope – hope and good wishes for Shirley's own family: for her well-being and that of her husband and their children.

Do you know the pain of being abused, or of a broken marriage, a failed relationship, hostilities between siblings, rivalry, jealousy? We all have excess baggage in one form or another in connection with our family life. Just as there is no perfect human being, so there can be no perfect family. The extraordinary part is that families function as well as they do, given the tensions of living in close proximity to people who can bring each other grief as well as joy!

> Everyone should be quick to listen, slow to speak and slow to become angry. For man's anger does not bring about the righteous life that God desires. Therefore get rid of all moral filth and the evil that is so prevalent, and humbly accept the word planted in you, which can save you. *James 1:19-21*

Working practice

Perhaps you've been on the receiving end at work – a colleague who spreads malicious gossip, the lashing of a caustic tongue, a belittling remark. Words can often be harmful and hurtful. Actions may be damaging too – an illicit relationship, an act of impulsive or premeditated violence. And don't forget the thought processes, the secrecy and deception that lead to disastrous words and actions.

I was the victim of malicious gossip when at college. A rumour started concerning one of the lecturers and his relationship with me. The whispers began with the idea that he favoured me above the rest of the group. My instinct was to hide! I wanted to retreat into an anonymous state of hibernation and wake up at the end of my course with the necessary qualifications to escape into the world of work. Fantasy. The reality was that the whispers became louder and, like the game of Chinese whispers, so distorted as to become near farce. But they were very painful – as well as being a web of lies.

> The tongue is a small part of the body, but it makes great boasts. Consider what a great forest is set on fire by a small spark. The tongue also is a fire, a world of evil among the parts of the body . . .
> *James 3:5-6*

Locals

Personal wrongs are one aspect. What about within the community? Some years ago our house was burgled. A window was smashed and the house ransacked. I returned home to find the front door wide open and a neighbour talking to the police. My young daughter was upset because a plant had been tipped off the window ledge where the forced entry had been made – and there was mud on the carpet. I made sure she didn't see our bedroom.

It transpired that three men had been to their mother's funeral and on the way home, after a few beers, decided to try their luck and find some electronic equipment that they could sell on for drug money. They were caught and served jail sentences. Did I have a sense of forgiveness towards them? No, I can't say I did. Shock was the first reaction, then dismay at the state of the house, then fear. My husband was out of the country on business, I had two small children to whom I needed to give calm attention – and I was afraid, mostly that the men might return, though most of the good pickings had already been taken. The fear abated after their arrest and trial. But it returned, albeit briefly, when I knew they had served their term and were out in the community again.

It was a long time ago and my attitude now is more one of pity than anything else. I don't know whether there was remorse on their part. There is more emphasis now on reparation, of offenders working for good in the community, of being counselled to consider the feelings of their victims; you even hear of healing relationships between offender and victim.

I don't believe that we can exercise forgiveness on a daily basis with unconditional love, grace and mercy unless we know the results of being forgiven by God. If we examine the lives of people who met Jesus and whose sins were forgiven, we see changed lives.

The dinner party

A woman came to Jesus and poured the most expensive perfume on him. His companions at dinner were incensed by such outrageous behaviour. What a waste of good perfume! What an immodest display by this disgraced and disgraceful woman of the streets! What an intrusion into the select gathering! How dare she! Jesus knew what his host was thinking and told the dinner guests a story.

Two men owed different amounts of money to a moneylender. Neither could repay, so the moneylender cancelled the debts of both. Which would be more grateful, Jesus asked. The answer was obvious. Why, the one who'd been let off the most, said Jesus' host. Right, said Jesus. And he went on to describe the scene at the dinner party. It seems that the host had not afforded Jesus the common courtesy of washing his feet when he arrived off the dusty streets, nor greeted him with a kiss. The woman had used perfume for washing, kissed Jesus, and generally lavished love and attention on him. 'I tell you,' Jesus said, 'Her many sins have been forgiven – for she loved me much. But he who has been forgiven little loves little.' Jesus said to the woman: 'Your faith has saved you; go in peace.'

In no way do I want to negate or underplay the damage that can be done to any of us through the wrongful act of a fellow human being. The reason we are asked to forgive is because God forgives us. Perhaps we haven't fully grasped what it meant to Jesus to lose everything for our sake, to give everything for our sake.

In arguably the most amazing words of Jesus on the cross he calls to his Father and says: 'Father, forgive them, for they don't know what they are doing.' Lord Jesus, you have done all that for me? From now on, I want to live for you and you alone. And if that means forgiving, then God help me, because I can't do it in my own strength.

I can't forgive myself

Sometimes we miss out on peace because we are unable to forgive ourselves. In this section on forgiving others, let's include ourselves. We may be carrying excess baggage. If we have asked God to forgive our sins, made a U-turn and are now on his road, there is no need for us to still be punishing ourselves – though so often we do! We may blame ourselves for what we have done wrong, we may blame ourselves for wrongs inflicted on us by others. With God's help we can learn to put the past behind us, remembering that, through Christ's work on the Cross, our guilt and shame have been buried by him – forever, and he accepts us, loves us and cherishes us . . . just as we are.

Culture of blame

Are you tempted to blame God and feel you can't forgive him for misfortunes in your life? In our blame culture we look for someone to accuse, for someone else to be responsible for whatever has cast us down. More than 42 chapters in the Bible relate the story of Job and how he dealt with an appalling sequence of tragedies that involved the deaths of all his children, the loss of his livelihood and a ghastly physical skin condition. 'Are you still holding on to your integrity?' asked his wife. 'Curse God and die!' Job, we read, 'did not sin by charging God with wrongdoing'. I'm not sure that I could undergo such testing times and not blame God.

Episcopal Director of the Anglican Institute in St Louis, USA, Rt Revd Michael Marshall wrote a book entitled *Just Like Him!* He suggested that trust and faith in and through suffering are founded upon the conviction that although the equation cannot be squared and resolved in history, it demands something of a courtroom vindication after life and beyond history – *at the last day*. He went on to say that if that is the case then God will be the advocate for those who have suffered and kept faith. So that begs a question of us. When our world falls apart, have we the faith to keep trusting God? Job, in his anguish, turned to God – in worship! Michael Marshall says that if we worship God only when things are going well . . . and curse and blaspheme him in the bad times of tears, our worship is little better than manipulation, therapy or blackmail. We need to remember that God, through Christ, is the suffering servant. He identifies with us in our suffering, in our troubles and hardships, because he has been there himself.

Sometimes, like the Psalmist, we may cry:

> Awake, O Lord! Why do you sleep? Rouse yourself! Do not reject us for ever. Why do you hide your face and forget our misery and oppression? Rise up and help us; redeem us because of your unfailing love. *Psalm 44:23-24, 26*

Blame's alternative

The antidote to blame and feeling hard done by, is trust and worship. Following the terrorist attacks of 11 September 2001 the words of Psalm 46 were much quoted.

> God is our refuge and strength, an ever present help in time of trouble. Therefore we will not fear, though the earth give way . . . Be still and know that I am God. I will be exalted among the nations. I will be exalted in the earth. The Lord Almighty is with us. *Psalm 46:1-2, 10-11*

The prayer of an old man reads:

> In you, O Lord, I have taken refuge, let me never be put to shame. Rescue me and deliver me . . . turn your ear to me and save me . . . be my rock of refuge to which I can always go . . . For you have been my hope, O Sovereign Lord, my confidence since my youth . . . I will ever praise you . . . I shall always have hope, I will praise you more and more . . . I will proclaim your mighty acts . . . I will proclaim your righteousness. O God you have taught me, and I will declare your marvellous deeds. *Psalm 71, selected verses*

Asaph found peace in God's presence:

> When my heart was grieved and my spirit embittered, I was senseless and ignorant; I was a brute beast before you. Yet I am always

with you; you hold me by my right hand. You guide me with your counsel, and afterwards you will take me into glory. Whom have I in heaven but you? And earth has nothing I desire besides you. My flesh and my heart may fail, but God is the strength of my heart and my portion for ever . . . It is good to be near God. *Psalm 73:21-26, 28a*

A vast canvas

When we have been wronged and find it hard to forgive, let's look at the bigger picture. Even where there are acts of extreme wickedness against the innocent, can we bring them to God and believe that he is just and he will judge everyone fairly? We may not see that happen in our lifetime, much as we might like the satisfaction of seeing justice done in front of our eyes. If we are able to let go of our indignation (righteous though it may be in our eyes), and lay down our 'rights', and come with humility before the God of justice and peace, we will experience his peace for ourselves, from which point we can walk on with a lighter tread – with him.

Let go and let God

Is it too glib to say that we are able to forgive when we know the results of being forgiven by God? What about extreme cruelty? And the deep, deep scars of an adult who was abused as a child? Jesus promises peace, the peace that passes all understanding. 'My peace I give to you, not as the world gives,' he says. Should God expect us to forgive other people when there is no remorse on their part?

Are we willing to try and forgive? Could we ask God for the gift of a forgiving spirit? Sometimes the burden of bitterness and hurt, anger and feelings of self-loathing can be so heavy that our bodies ache with the hurt. If we can let go of the burden it is possible that, in time, our bodies relax and healing will wash over us. It may take a long time for the bruises to disappear, but if there is a willingness to try, there is hope. Jesus Christ knew the burdens that people carry – the burden of their own shortcomings, but also the burdens inflicted by other people and by circumstances. 'Come to me,' he invited, 'all of you who are weary and burdened, and I will give you rest.' And he used an analogy from the farming business: 'Take my yoke upon you and learn from me, for I am gentle and humble in heart, and you will find rest for your souls.' Perhaps a starting point is to find a trusted friend, who knows the peace that Christ brings, with whom you could share something of your burden.

Jesus gives us the opportunity to begin again with God. Forgiveness is at the heart of the Christian faith but when trust has been broken, when wounds are deep and painful, forgiveness is very, very tough. While God forgives and forgets, we find it hard to forgive, let alone forget. Even when there has been forgiveness, we are wary, watching and wanting to make sure we're not hurt again. Love hurts. And, yes, forgiveness hurts. We know that because of Christ. He was willing to give until it hurt to the point of death. God was willing to forgive till it hurt. Am I willing to give what I have received: love, forgiveness, peace, joy? If I let go and let God, I can leave humiliation, indignation, anger and resentment with him. When circumstances are such that those who have wronged us seem not to show any sign of remorse, we can leave it with God. We are not asked to pass sentence on them but to forgive them. Judgement is God's domain. Can we leave it with him? If we can, we will begin to feel a sense of release.

Points to ponder

Joseph in the Old Testament is chronicled in great detail and spans his life from a teenage show-off to his death nearly 100 years later. It could match any family saga of modern fact or fiction and has an extraordinarily contemporary ring to it. We read of favouritism, hatred, jealousy, deceit, cruelty, grief, attempted seduction, false imprisonment, broken promises, famine and fear. But out of all the mess and misery came humility, hope, provision and reconciliation.

Bible reading

Take time, if you can, to read the whole story from Genesis 37 through to Genesis 50. It's a gripping read!

Genesis 37:1-11

- Joseph was in trouble from the word go. Why? *(verses 2-3)*
- How did Joseph make a bad situation worse? *(verses 5-9)*
- What was the result of Joseph's cocky attitude? *(verses 11 and 18)*

The spoilt teenager, who hadn't yet learned the art of tact and diplomacy, was set upon by his brothers, who plotted to kill him. Plans changed, and after dumping him in an empty well, they rid themselves of their hated brother by selling him to a group of travelling merchants. Needing to give an explanation to their father for the absent Joseph, they concocted a story of a ferocious animal setting upon the lad and killing him. To add insult to injury, they killed a goat and splattered its blood on the special coat Joseph had been given by his father, and took the wretched garment to Jacob.

Take a few moments to imagine how Joseph felt at different stages:

- when he went to look for his brothers. *(verses 12-17)*
- when he saw their looks of hatred. *(verses 19-20)*
- when his brothers stripped him. *(verse 23)*
- when they threw him into the well and then sat down to their picnic. *(verse 24)*
- when he was pulled out of the well – did he hope his punishment was over. *(verse 28)*
- when he saw money handed over to the Ishmaelites. *(verse 28)*
- when he was plonked on a camel and found himself on his way to Egypt. *(verse 28)*
- Did he physically look back at his brothers and his home land, mentally look back at his life and take stock? Emotionally, how did he feel?

Once in Egypt, things went from bad to better then worse for Joseph. Yet again, money changed hands as the captain of Pharoah's guard, Potiphar, bought him and set him to work for him. He did well at his job and became Potiphar's personal attendant.

- Read Genesis 39:1-6. Notice the difference God made! How many times is the Lord mentioned? These verses suggest that during his journey to Egypt Joseph had plenty of time to think and to sort himself out with God. Although he had been sinned against, he had had time to acknowledge before God his own shortcomings. Rather than indulge in self-pity, or righteous anger, he turned something negative into a positive. Clearly he was prepared to work hard at his job, was trustworthy and competent. He was also good-looking . . .
- Read Genesis 39:7-19. Trouble! Just as Joseph's life was beginning

to look rosier, he had hassle from the boss's wife. He repeatedly refused her advances but, with the anger of a woman scorned and spurned, she created a rumpus, accusing Joseph of attempted rape.

Joseph was thrown into prison, his integrity intact but his reputation in apparent ruins. Yet . . . read Genesis 39: 2-3, 5, 9, 21-23. Who was with Joseph? What difference did it make to Joseph, his work, his responsibilities, his attitude? What difference might a right relationship with God make in my life?

The Lord was with Joseph in prison, but, thanks to the broken promise of a fellow prisoner to put in a good word for Joseph, he stayed in prison for a further two years. Christianity is a faith, rather than a religion. It is a relationship built on trust. When times are hard, the wishy-washy weak can't cope and opt out. Jesus warned his disciples that following him was going to be tough. Joseph's faith was put to the test over and over again – and he came out shining. It is in difficult times that we find out how strong our foundation is. No wonder Jesus told us to build our lives on the rock of his word, rather than on sinking sand!

Thought for the day

When God has first place in our lives, even the most awful events can be turned to good. Faith requires a solid base on which to build; otherwise we'll crumble beneath the crushing blows that may come our way.

Further reading: Genesis 42-50

What is the place of repentance, reparation, reconciliation and restoration in our relationships with those who have wronged us, with those whom we have wronged, and with God?

Memorise

Trust in the Lord with all your heart, and lean not on your own understanding; in all your ways acknowledge him, and he will make your paths straight. Do not be wise in your own eyes; fear the Lord and shun evil. *Proverbs 3:5, 6-7*

Prayer

Father God,
>   may I learn that however badly I may have been treated by others,
>   it is not my place to judge them.

Teach me how to live in harmony with those close to me,
>   to turn to you in repentance for my wrongdoing
>   even when reeling from the wrongs against me.

May I learn, as Joseph did,
>   to put my life in your hands,
>   to be willing to serve you as my Lord,
>   and to know the joy of a restored relationship with you
>   and with other people.

Amen.

Chapter 9

The way forward

The pilgrim path

All rising to great place is by a winding stair. *Francis Bacon 1561-1626 (English lawyer, courtier, philosophist and essayist)*

Once we have done the U-turn of repentance, and been forgiven, we are on God's pilgrim path, and have a passport to heaven, but beware! We are still going to make mistakes. We still let other people down and thus let God down. Our old human nature still wants to rear its ugly head and, at times, will get the better of us. So what do we do? Slump into despair, flagellate ourselves, give up the struggle? No. Let's recognise that Christianity is a faith. 'It can't be lived by logic,' says Roger Pearce, minister of Northwood Hills Evangelical Church, 'The Christian life is supernatural. The Spirit helps us in our weakness. We are utterly, totally dependent on the Spirit.'

Jesus Christ knows our weaknesses. Having told the disciples that he was going to die, Jesus reassured them in their panic and sorrow.

If you love me, you will obey what I command. And I will ask the Father, and he will give you another Counsellor to be with you for ever – the Spirit of truth . . . If anyone loves me, he will obey my teaching . . . The Counsellor, the Holy Spirit, whom the Father will send in my name, will teach you all things and will remind you of everything I have said to you. Peace I leave with you; my peace I give you. I do not give to you as the world gives. Do not let your hearts be troubled and do not be afraid. *John 14:15-17, 23, 26-27*

Let's keep short accounts with God – and with other people. He has forgiven us our sins but when we let him down we need to own up – on a daily basis, say we're sorry and ask him to help us, by his Spirit, to live his way. How do we discern that way?

Jesus said: 'I am the way and the truth and the life. No one comes to the Father except through me.' *John 14:6*

Words of life

Let's immerse ourselves in him! God has given us the written word and the living word – the Bible and Jesus Christ. Both show us God's way to live. It's the way of peace and of freedom. Freedom within bounds – bounds to protect rather than prohibit. As we search the scriptures and put into practice what we discover our lives will become illuminated by the light of Christ. A friend described her light as a rather feeble pilot light. Sometimes it may seem like a wavering candle, blown by a chill draught that wants to snuff it out. But as long as there is a willingness to allow the Spirit to do his work and transform us, our flame will begin to burn more confidently because our dependence is on God whose reliability, faithfulness and constancy are unequalled because they are perfect and entire.

Just before Moses died, he reminded the people about God's pattern for living and its benefits. He concluded:

> Take to heart all the words I have solemnly declared to you this day . . .
> They are not just idle words for you – they are your life.
> *Deuteronomy 32:46-47*

> Your word, O Lord, is eternal . . . Your word is a lamp to my feet and a light to my path. *Psalm 119:89, 105*

Throughout history those words were heard, at times adhered to, but often ignored. And then God sent his Son, Jesus Christ, the Word in human form.

> In the beginning was the Word, and the Word was with God, and the Word was God . . . He was in the world, and though the world was made through him, the world did not recognise him. He came to that which was his own, but his own did not receive him. Yet to all who received him, to those who believed in his name, he gave the right to become children of God . . . The Word became flesh and lived for a while among us. We have seen his glory, the glory of the one and only Son, who came from the Father, full of grace and truth.
> *John 1:1, 10-12, 14*

The apostle, John, testified to Jesus Christ in a letter:

> That which was from the beginning, which we have heard, which we have seen with our eyes, which we have looked at and our hands have touched – this we proclaim concerning the Word of life. The life appeared; we have seen it and testify to it, and we proclaim to you

the eternal life, which was with the Father and has appeared to us. We proclaim to you what we have seen and heard, so that you also may have fellowship with us. And our fellowship is with the Father and with his Son, Jesus Christ. *1 John 1:1-3*

Interdependence

We were not born to be independent. As babies we were dependent on parents and carers. Parents are called to be human guardians on behalf of God. Gradually, throughout childhood, into adolescence and towards adulthood, the child develops into a person who becomes less dependent on those guardians. The child has been prepared for its role as an adult, ready to make its own choices and take its own decisions. We need to remember, however, that God is a relational God who created us for company – with each other and with himself. Interdependence, rather than independence, is what we should be experiencing. Increasingly, more people are living alone, but relationships are still of paramount importance.

It is illogical and foolhardy to expect to be independent as followers of Jesus Christ. It is hard to live effectively as his disciples in our own company and in our own strength. God, in his fatherly goodness, wants to lavish his love on us, he longs to guide our steps, his desire is for open communication between his forgiven people and himself. God's forgiven, adopted children, Jesus Christ's brothers and sisters need the friendship and support of each other. Like sibling relationships in any family, peace and harmony have to be worked at; opting out of Christian fellowship isn't helpful. However flawed the Christian community may be its members need each other!

My Lord and my God

Jesus Christ, the Word, is described in the Bible as our Saviour (through whom we receive forgiveness of sins), our brother, our friend, our priest who is our link to God. Above all, for his forgiven followers, he must be Lord. Do we allow Jesus to be Lord of every aspect of our life, or do we like to hang on to the old sinful nature for some bits? If Jesus is not Lord of all, he is not Lord at all.

Jesus knew how hard his disciples would find life without him there as their friend and brother. He assured them that he would never leave them because God would send the Holy Spirit to be their helper. If you have a hard task to do, it's easier with two! The trellis on our fence blew down in a gale. For one of us to have fixed it would have been very difficult; with two, the job was soon done. The Holy Spirit is our counsellor, someone in whom we can confide, someone to consult when we're needing God's wisdom. He is our teacher; as we study God's written Word, the Holy Spirit teaches us what it means and how to live it out. He is our constant companion because he lives in the lives of the forgiven. And given the opportunity, through our willing obedience to the Word, he is the fruit producer, producing good things that are worthy of the Christ for whom we live.

Christians are learners – and always will be. In order to learn, we have to be taught and we have to study. Swotting hard the night before an exam rarely pays dividends; it is the steady, disciplined work day by day that will bring results. Jesus Christ was dependent on his Father; he prayed, he studied the scriptures, he worshipped with others. Who are we to do less?

Points to ponder

If we turn to follow Jesus Christ, we must be prepared to live his way – which doesn't come naturally! The challenges are immense.

Bible reading: Luke 6:27-49

Look at what we are called to do:

- Love your enemies!
- Do good – not just to your pals, but to those who hate you!
- Bless people – the ones who curse you!
- Pray for people – including those who ill-treat you!
- Give – be generous!
- Show mercy – following God's example!
- Don't judge people.
- Don't condemn others.
- Forgive other people.

A tall order? Definitely. How can we do such things? Only by having our lives solidly placed on the right foundation.

Notice what Jesus tells us to do in verses 46-49.

- **Come.** We need to come to Jesus – his invitation is there but we have to accept it – or reject it. When we come, what's next?
- **Listen.** Some of us may come, take a look but let our minds and eyes wander. We can't expect to make progress unless we listen to our Lord. But that's not all.
- **Obey.** His words are not empty; their substance is life itself. We may come and listen but if we don't obey Jesus and live God's way, we're heading for trouble, as this story reveals. Moreover, we miss out on the blessings that God wants to give us.

Notice that Jesus doesn't say that following him will be sunshine and roses. It is important that each follower of Jesus realises the cost; storms will come, in various forms, and batter us. We will face temptation, we will know suffering, we may face persecution – Jesus did, and he calls us to follow him. The good news is that, if our lives are founded on that solid rock, no matter how bashed and battered our circumstances, the house that is our faith will stand firm.

It is arrogant to suppose that we can be disciples, with all that that entails, without the Word being a strong component of our daily lives.

Thought for the day

We used to sing these words: 'Read your Bible, pray every day, if you want to grow.' This is not a legal requirement but common sense tells us that it is the best way to stand firm on the rock.

Memorise

Since you have accepted Christ Jesus as Lord, live in union with him. Keep your roots deep in him, build your lives on him, and become stronger in your faith, as you were taught. And be filled with thanksgiving. *Colossians 2:6-7.*

Prayer

Lord Jesus,
    I want to go forward in my walk with you.
I can't do it alone.
May my gratitude for all you have done for me
      give me the desire to want to commune with you
      through prayer and the Word on a daily basis,
      so that I can grow and learn how to live out
      the forgiven and forgiving life that you have shown me.
Amen.

Chapter 10

Living the forgiven life

Follow the leader

We've played it with our children and I used to play it as a child: Follow the leader. The leader sets off round the garden or down the road, the followers have to follow exactly where he leads. We look to see where he puts his feet, we jump over the same obstacles, stoop to smell the same flowers, and so on. To get sidetracked, go down blind alleys, take short cuts . . . is not playing the game.

Christians are called by Christ to follow *him*, not our own inclinations, the latest fad, political leader or superstar. It is as we keep our eyes fixed on Jesus and follow him that we will learn his ways and become more like him.

Let's learn to see things his way, to treat people as he would. Let's put self on the back-burner and Christ to the fore! This will help so much in the struggle to forgive because we will do it, not in our strength, but in his.

It's tempting but would be inappropriate to try and give a 'How to forgive . . .' list of steps to take. The blueprint for learning to forgive others as God in Christ has forgiven us, lies in his Word, the Bible. Jesus Christ is our pattern. His Spirit within the believer lights up the way ahead; his Church, the body of flawed but learning fellow believers, is the source of mutual encouragement. So let's go forward with courage and anticipation; the Christian life is an adventure with challenges, joys and trials. I leave it to God and his Word to point us in the right direction:

In our thoughts

Whatever is true, whatever is noble, whatever is right, whatever is pure, whatever is lovely, whatever is admirable –if anything is excellent or praiseworthy – think about such things . . . And the God of peace will be with you. *Philippians 4:8*

In our speech

Let your conversation be always full of grace. *Colossians 4:6*

Everyone should be quick to listen, slow to speak and slow to become angry, for man's anger does not bring about the righteous life that God desires. *James 1:19-20*

In our behaviour

Produce fruit in keeping with repentance. *Matthew 3:8*

The fruit of the Spirit is love, joy, peace, patience, kindness, goodness, faithfulness, gentleness and self-control . . . Those who belong to Christ Jesus have crucified the sinful nature with its passions and desires. Since we live by the Spirit, let us keep in step with the Spirit. *Galatians 5:22-25*

As God's chosen people, holy and dearly loved, clothe yourselves with compassion, kindness, humility, gentleness and patience. Bear with each other and forgive whatever grievances you may have against one another. Forgive as the Lord forgave you. And over all these virtues put on love, which binds them all together in perfect unity. Let the peace of Christ rule in your hearts, since as members of one body you were called to peace. And be thankful. Let the word of Christ dwell in you richly . . . And whatever you do, whether in word or deed, do it in the name of the Lord Jesus, giving thanks to God the Father through him. *Colossians 3:12-17*

Be wise!

Who is wise and understanding among you? Let him show it by his good life, by deeds done in the humility that comes from wisdom. But if you harbour bitter envy and selfish ambition in your hearts, do not boast about it or deny the truth. Such 'wisdom' does not come down from heaven but is earthly, unspiritual, of the devil. For where you have envy and selfish ambition, there you find disorder and every evil practice. But the wisdom that comes from heaven is first of all pure; then peace-loving, considerate, submissive, full of mercy and good fruit, impartial and sincere. Peacemakers who sow in peace raise a harvest of righteousness. *James 3:13-18*

THE RESULTS OF FORGIVENESS

Freedom

Now that you have been set free from sin and have become slaves to God, the benefit you reap leads to holiness, and the result is eternal life. For the wages of sin is death, but the gift of God is eternal life in Christ Jesus our Lord. *Romans 6:22-23*

Where the Spirit of the Lord is, there is freedom. *2 Corinthians 3:17*

It is for freedom that Christ has set us free . . . But do not use your freedom to indulge the sinful nature; rather, serve one another in love. *Galatians 5:1, 13*

He has rescued us from the dominion of darkness and brought us into the kingdom of the Son he loves, in whom we have redemption, the forgiveness of sins. *Colossians 1:13-14*

Live as free men, but do not use your freedom as a cover-up for evil; live as servants of God. *1 Peter 2:16*

Grace

From the fullness of his grace we have all received one blessing after another. *John 1:16*

We believe that it is through the grace of our Lord Jesus that we are saved. *Acts 15:11*

. . . his grace given you in Christ Jesus. For in him you have been enriched in every way. *1 Corinthians 1:4-5*

God said: 'My grace is sufficient for you, for my power is made perfect in weakness'. *2 Corinthians 12:9*

In him we have redemption through his blood, the forgiveness of sins, in accordance with the riches of God's grace that he lavished on us. *Ephesians 1:7*

May our Lord Jesus Christ himself and God our Father, who loved us and by his grace gave us eternal encouragement and good hope, encourage your hearts and strengthen you in every good deed and word. *2 Thessalonians 2:16-17*

Let us approach the throne of grace with confidence, so that we may receive mercy and find grace to help us in our time of need. *Hebrews 4:16*

Joy

Do not be afraid. I bring you good news of great joy that will be for all the people. Today in the town of David, a Saviour has been born to you, he is Christ the Lord. *Luke 2:10-11*

Though you have not seen Jesus Christ, you love him . . . you believe in him and are filled with an inexpressible and glorious joy, for you are receiving the goal of your faith, the salvation of your souls. *1 Peter 1:8-9*

Love divine, all loves excelling,
Joy of heaven, to earth come down.

Charles Wesley, 1707-1788 (co-founder of Methodism and prolific composer of hymns)

Praise and thankfulness

I will praise you for ever for what you have done. *Psalm 52:9*

Give thanks to the Lord for his unfailing love. *Psalm 107:21*

Just as you received Christ Jesus as Lord, continue to live in him, rooted and built up in him, strengthened in the faith as you were taught, and overflowing with thankfulness. *Colossians 2:6-7*

Praise be to the God and Father of our Lord Jesus Christ! In his great mercy he has given us new birth into a living hope through the resurrection of Jesus Christ from the dead, and into an inheritance that can never perish, spoil or fade – kept in heaven for you. *1 Peter 1:3-4*

Peace

Jesus said: 'Peace I leave with you; my peace I give you. I do not give to you as the world gives. Do not let your hearts be troubled and do not be afraid.' *John 14:27*

The peace of God, which transcends all understanding, will guard your hearts and your minds in Christ Jesus. *Philippians 4:7*

Restored relationship with God

To all who received him, to those who believed in his name, he gave the right to become children of God. *John 1:12*

Those who are led by the Spirit of God are sons of God. For you did not receive a spirit that makes you a slave again to fear, but you received the Spirit of sonship. And by him we cry, 'Abba' (Daddy) . . . We are God's children, heirs of God and co-heirs with Christ. *Romans 8:14-17*

How great is the love the Father has lavished on us, that we should be called children of God! *1 John 3:1*

Everyone who believes that Jesus is the Christ is born of God. *1 John 5:1*

A changed life

I have been crucified with Christ and I no longer live, but Christ lives in me. The life I live in the body, I live by faith in the Son of God, who loved me and gave himself for me. *Galatians 2:19-20*

The fruit of the Spirit is love, joy, peace, patience, kindness, goodness, faithfulness, gentleness and self-control . . . those who belong to Christ Jesus have crucified the sinful nature with its passions and desires. Since we live by the Spirit, let us keep in step with the Spirit. *Galatians 5:22-25*

Prepare your minds for action; be self-controlled; set your hope fully on the grace to be given you when Jesus Christ is revealed. As obedient children, do not conform to the evil desires you had when you lived in ignorance. But just as he who called you is holy, so be holy in all you do. *1 Peter 1:13-15*

Points to ponder

Give yourself time to reflect on the attributes, purpose and person of Jesus Christ, as we come to the end of this book on forgiveness. Consider how he could change your life today and for all time.

Bible reading: John 1:1-18

These words are often read at carol services around Christmas time, often with the listeners standing. They are amazing words that focus on Jesus Christ. Not only do we have the written Word of God – the Bible, but we have the living Word of God – Jesus Christ.

- Jesus, as part of the triune Godhead, has been present since the beginning of time. *(verses 1-3)* Have a look at Genesis 1:26 and notice the plural, 'we'.

- Compare verses 4-5 with John 10:10, John 11:25, John 6:35 and John 14:6; also John 8:12.
    How much 'life' and 'light' is there inyour life?

- Have you recognised Jesus for who he is? *(verses 10-11)* Have you received him?

- What must we do to receive Jesus? *(verse 12)* See also John 3:16.

- What is the new relationship believers have with God? *(verses 12-13)*

- Because Jesus lived as a human being we have a portrait of God's character and attributes. Jesus is described as being 'full of grace and truth' *(verse 14)*. What does it mean to you to have God's grace – undeserved and immeasurable love – showered on you?

Jesus was 'full of truth'. We are used to hearing about politicians being, 'economical with the truth', a euphemism for being downright untruthful! How honest are we? How does being 'economical with the truth' adversely affect relationships at home, at work, at school? Deceit is a label that could never be pinned on Jesus. Look at John 14:6. On innumerable occasions Jesus started his talks with the words, 'I tell you the truth . . .' What confidence this gives us! How important it is to know that the one who teaches us how to pray, who offers us forgiveness, and tells us to ask God to help us forgive others, is speaking the truth, the whole truth and nothing but the truth! If it were not so, our faith would be founded on doubt, deception and duplicity and end in disillusionment and disaster.

- Read John 21:24-25. John wanted his readers to know the truth – Jesus, the Truth, – so he puts in this underlining statement at the end of his Gospel so that there can be no doubt as to the validity of what he has recorded. See also 1 John 1:1-4 – notice what John writes: We have heard . . . We have seen . . . We have looked at . . . Our hands have touched . . . We proclaim concerning the Word of life (Jesus) We have seen (the Life) . . . we testify to it . . . we proclaim to you the eternal life . . . (the Life) appeared to us . . .

We proclaim to you what we have seen and heard . . . why? In verse 3 John is so sure of Jesus that he wants nothing better than for others to share him too! The result is joy! *(verse 4b)*

Thought for the day

Confidence, encouragement, commitment, assurance, come to believers as they come close to Jesus. That happens through reading the written Word about the living Word. That is the way forward.

Memorise

My friends, keep building yourselves up on your most sacred faith. Pray in the power of the Holy Spirit, and keep yourselves in the love of God, as you wait for our Lord Jesus Christ in his mercy to give you eternal life. *Jude 20-21.*

Prayer

Lord Jesus, you have given your all for me.
May I be prepared to give my all to you.
Amen.

. . . And finally

Faith operates in an imperfect world; only by putting our trust in God can we begin to see some answers to our questions, our doubts lessen and our picture broaden. My investigations into the subject of forgiveness have hardly touched the surface; I hope that, like me, you will want to investigate further, but take that first life-changing step of saying, 'Father, forgive me . . .'

I suggest that as we turn our backs on our former life and turn to God for forgiveness we will start to sense his peace which, in turn, will enable us to live life in its fullness – as God intended: forgiven, learning to forgive and free to live out our brief blip on earth with purpose, peace and the privilege of being a tiny but significant part of God's vast canvas that spans space, history and eternity.

> We always thank God, the Father of our Lord Jesus Christ, when we pray for you, because we have heard of your faith in Christ Jesus . . . We have not stopped praying for you and asking God to fill you with the knowledge of his will through all spiritual wisdom and understanding. And we pray this in order that you may live a life worthy of the Lord and may please him in every way, bearing fruit in every good work, growing in the knowledge of God, being strengthened with all power according to his glorious might so that you may have great endurance and patience, and joyfully giving thanks to the Father, who has qualified you to share in the inheritance of the saints in the kingdom of light. For he has rescued us from the dominion of darkness and brought us into the kingdom of the Son he loves, in whom we have redemption, the forgiveness of sins.
> *Colossians 1:3, 9-14*